CONNECTING THE DOTS

FOR EVERYDAY PEOPLE

LIVING YOUR LIFE

ONE PRODUCTIVE DECISION AT A TIME

Volume I

<u>IMMEDIATE NEEDS</u>

Eric D. Eason

NO MATTER WHAT STAGE OF LIFE YOU ARE IN EVERYTHING IS CONTINGENT UPON YOUR NEXT DECISION!

ISBN # 978-0-615-32125-7

Copyright in 2010 by Eric Eason
All rights reserved. No part of this publication may be reproduced, distributed or transmitted in any form or by any means without the prior written consent of the publisher.

www.youarenextpublishing.com

eric@youarenextpublishing.com

Editors: Mae Morris and Paul Altese
Mays Printing Company, Inc.
15800 Livernois Avenue
Detroit, MI 48238
313.861.1900
www.maysprinting.com

Cover Design by:
Beyond Horizon, LLC
313.468.5303
Jason_flowers@msn.com

Back Cover Photo by:
I.C.U. Photo Gallery
313.285.7794
Icuphotogallery.com

Marketing by:
Alternative Management and Marketing Group, LLC
313.473.8260
I.nero@sbcglobal.net

Business Consultant:
Henderson Jones Consulting
240.293.6219
henderson_jones@hotmail.com

Disclaimer

Connecting The Dots is not a substitute for directly communicating to a professional service provider, i.e., clinical therapist, professional counselor or life coach. Connecting The Dots may increase your level of participation with your current professional service provider or become the catalyst for you to obtain a professional service provider as a result of attempting to connect some of your dots in your life as you engage in the series Connecting The Dots.

SPECIAL ACKNOWLEDGEMENTS

Special thanks to the following persons:

To the Trinity: God the Father, God the Son and God the Holy Spirit. In God, we move, breathe and have our being. Absolutely nothing occurs without God's consent… "And we know that all things work for the good of those who love God who have been called according to his purpose.

To my mother: "Princess" Sadie Mae Eason (the best counselor ever). I thank you for making the decision to allow me to live during a challenging time in your life. I thank you for the way in which you raised me. I thank you for the countless hours of sharing with me your pearls of wisdom and demonstration of unconditional love. Most importantly, I thank you for introducing me to Jesus Christ.

To my wife: Christal Eason - I thank you for introducing me to our church ministry. I thank you for allowing me to be a father. I thank you for the time that you had invested in me to grow as a husband.

To my children: Michael and Justice - I thank God for allowing me to be your father and providing sound and biblical instructions as I was learning God's word myself.

To my family: Joseph, Lorenzo, Alphonso, Lucille and Demone - I thank God for the special bond that we will forever share.

To my spiritual parents: Bishop Edgar L. Vann and Elder Sheila R. Vann at Second Ebenezer Church in Detroit, Michigan - I thank God for commissioning the both of you to be the under shepherds for me and my family from this side of heaven.

To my former clients: I thank you for the countless hours and the many years of entrusting me with the most sensitive areas of your past to offer you sound recommendations to stabilize your present in preparation for your future.

To my everyday people: Henderson Jones, LaVell Nero, Robert Bankston, Jr., Rev. Anthony C. Russell and Pastor William Pacey - I thank you for your prayers and your support during my years of transformation to be the God-Man I am today:

As we know God works through signs and wonders. I thank God for the sign of sunshine. Sunshine represents that a new day has began – equivalent to a new chapter in your life is about to be written.

Lamentations 3:22 -23 "It is of the Lord's mercies that we are not consumed, for his compassions fail not. They are new every morning: great is thy faithfulness." - KJV

DESCRIPTION OF CONNECTING THE DOTS

Remember in primary school your teacher probably distributed the Connect-The-Dots handouts for you to complete as means of a reward for demonstrating positive behavior or used as a tool of de-escalation if you were a disruptive child.

Connect-The-Dots consisted of a series of dots beginning from the number (1) to whatever the numerical series ended. The process was for you to use a pencil and draw from the start or point of origin which was the lowest number to the next ascending number to the next ascending number and so forth to the last number in that numerical series. You had to follow that specific order to get the correct results. The results were an image or picture that was created from connecting each dot in the order it was suppose to occur.

If you connected out of order then the image or picture would be skewed or distorted. As a result you would have to reassess where you went wrong in drawing your lines from one dot to the next. After you identify the error then you would use your eraser to make the necessary corrections so that you could reconnect the lines to each dot to obtain the original image or picture.

The only instruction for Connect-The-Dots handout is to follow "the order" of the numerical series. Connect-The-Dots handouts can be parallel to the vehicle called "Life". To life there is an order. I heard many definitions of the word (order) but I have been arrested by Bishop Edgar Vann's definition, "Order is the regulation of a prevailing course or an arrangement of things that reinforces the intent of God."

However many people go through life not completely aware of the importance of following order. There are a large percentage of people who wants to do whatever they want to do regardless of how their actions may affect their lives or the lives of others. They refuse to go through the numerical series – which is equivalent to making one good decision at a time.

Furthermore many people go through life using a pen to make all of their life decisions. Therefore when they realize they have made an error they appear to be incapable of rectifying the problem because they used an instrument that leaves a permanent mark - ink. Instead a person should use a pencil. The pencil is symbolic of God's grace and mercy. The pencil allows you to make corrections once you can honestly identify what and where did you go wrong.

This book will challenge the reader to explore each current situation in their life and how past decisions have affected their current decision and how their current decision will affect future decisions. In other words, if you have currently made a poor decision then your next decision is already in jeopardy of not yielding a positive outcome. Therefore, choose wisely so that your next decision will be in order to the final image of your life.

INTRODUCTION TO YOUR GUIDE

As for man's recognition on this side of heaven, I think I can best serve you with my credentials and expertise if I provide you with a brief snapshot of my career portfolio. In addition, if the reader, especially a person in the human service field favors this style of resume writing then by all means tailor it to meet your needs.

EDUCATION:

DEGREES	**FIELD OF CONCENTRATION**	**UNIVERSITY**
Master of Arts	Counseling Education	Wayne State University
Bachelor of Arts	Political Science	Wilberforce University

PROFESSIONAL LICENSES AND CERTIFICATIONS:

- Licensed Minister of the Gospel of Jesus Christ under Bishop Edgar L. Vann
- Limited License Professional Counselor (LLPC)
- Certified Advanced Addictions Counselor
- International Reciprocity Addictions Counselor
- Certified Prison In-reach Trainer

CLINICAL EXPERIENCE:

MODALITIES	**SUBJECT**	**SPECIFIERS**
INDIVIDUAL THERAPY:	Mental Health	Cognitive Impairment
	Emotional	Affective Domain (feelings)
	Behavioral	Cognitive functioning influencing behavior

GROUP THERAPY:	Clinical		Cognitive Functioning
	Life Skills		Daily Functioning
	Socialization		Healthy Interactions
FAMILY THERAPY:	Stabilization		Focuses on Prevention
	Reunification		Focuses on Intervention
MENTORING:	Guidance/Direction		Role Modeling

SPECIAL TOPICS

Substance Abuse	Sexual Abuse	Anger Management
Grief and Loss	Domestic Violence	Depression

SPECIAL POPULATIONS

Mental Health (adults and juveniles) – hospitalization, residential and community mental health services.

Substance Abusers (male and female adults, juveniles) – residential and outpatient services.

Inmates (adult males) – County Jails and State Correctional Facilities.

Ex-offenders (male and female adults) – Prison Reentry Programs.

Juveniles (male and female teens) – residential mental health services.

TABLE OF CONTENTS

DOT #1 – RESIDENCY: EVEN BATMAN HAD THE BAT CAVE.

DOT #2 – FINANCES: MONEY IS NOT EVERYTHING, BUT IT HELPS TO HAVE SOME.

DOT #3 – TRANSPORTATION: KEEPS YOU MOVING.

DOT #4 – LEGAL: YOU CAN NOT LIVE IF YOU ARE CONSTANTLY RUNNING.

DOT #5 – MEDICAL: WHAT IS MY BODY REALLY SAYING?

DOT #1

RESIDENCY

EVEN BATMAN HAD THE BAT CAVE

DOT #1-A   MAN VERSUS NATURE

DOT #1-B - WHO ARE YOU LIVING WITH?

DOT #1-C - WHAT IS THE TYPE OF RESIDENCY?

DOT #1-D   WHERE IS THE LOCATION?

DOT #1-E   HOME OWNERSHIP

DOT #1-F   REFINANCE

DOT #1- G   HOME OWNERS INSURANCE

DOT #1 H   HOME IMPROVEMENTS

DOT #1 I   RENTAL

MAN VERSUS NATURE

What is shelter?

_____
_____
_____
_____

Define residency.

_____
_____
_____
_____

If applicable, describe the circumstances which led you to be homeless.

_____
_____
_____
_____

How did you respond to your homeless status?

_____
_____
_____
_____

Describe the circumstances of a family member or friend that was homeless.

___

How did you respond to this person's homeless status?

___

What support, if any did you render to this person?

___

Describe your experience visiting a homeless shelter.

___

CONNECTING DOT (1-A)

What does your picture look like in this area?

_____
_____
_____
_____
_____
_____
_____
_____

What did you learn about yourself?

_____
_____
_____
_____
_____
_____
_____
_____

CONNECTING DOT (1-A)

What, if any, steps will you begin to implement to draw a different picture to improve this area of your life?

WHO ARE YOU LIVING WITH?

SELECT AND EXPLAIN WHO YOU LIVE WITH:

The following selections are …

Self	Both Parents	Siblings	Friend
Spouse	Father – only	Brother–only	Other
Spouse and children	Mother - only	Sister-only	

_____
_____
_____
_____

The advantages of living with this person:

_____
_____
_____
_____

The disadvantages of living with this person if any:

_____
_____
_____
_____

WHAT IS THE TYPE OF RESIDENCY?

SELECT AND EXPLAIN YOUR RESIDENCY:

The following selections are …

Mobile Home	Apartment/Loft	Single Home	Duplex
Brownstone	Townhouse	Condominium	Other

_____

_____

_____

_____

What is meant by the phrase "A house is not a home?"

_____

_____

_____

_____

What is meant by the phrase "A family that prays together, stays together?"

_____

_____

_____

_____

Describe the interior of your living room.

_____

_____

_____

_____

Describe the interior of your dining room.

_____

_____

_____

_____

Describe the interior of your kitchen.

_____

_____

_____

_____

Describe the interior of your entertainment room.

_____

_____

_____

_____

Describe the interior of your bedroom.

_____
_____
_____
_____
_____

Describe the interior of your child or children's rooms.

_____
_____
_____
_____
_____

Describe the interior of your guest room.

_____
_____
_____
_____
_____

Describe the interior of your bathroom.

_____
_____
_____
_____
_____

Describe the interior of your study/home office.

Describe the interior of your basement.

What is your favorite room and why?

What is your least favorite room and why?

Describe the exterior of your residency.

_____
_____
_____
_____

List any changes that you will implement to any exterior parts/areas and why.

_____
_____
_____
_____

List several chores you have difficulty in completing and why?

_____
_____
_____
_____

How is this residency different from your childhood residency?

_____
_____
_____
_____

CONNECTING DOTS (1B-1C)

What does your picture look like in this area?

What did you learn about yourself?

What, if any, steps will you begin to implement to draw a different picture to improve this area of your life?

WHERE IS THE LOCATION?

My _____ is located in a/an…

Urban Area/ Suburban Area/ Rural Area called _____

The advantages of this location/area are:

_____
_____
_____
_____
_____
_____
_____

The disadvantages of this location/area are:

_____
_____
_____
_____
_____
_____
_____

Describe the location of the following landmarks - include more than the address.

Example - What is the address and location of your local police department?
   1300 Beaubien Street; Detroit, MI 48226; located next to Greek Town

Emergency Civil Service

Where is the location of your local police department?

_____

_____

Where is the location of your local fire department?

_____

_____

Where is the location of your local hospital?

_____

_____

Government Buildings

Where is the location of your federal building?

_____

_____

Where is the location of your state building?

_____

_____

Where is the location of your local city hall/municipal building?

_____

_____

Where is the location of your voting precinct?

_____

_____

Public Utilities

Where is the location of your gas company?

_____

_____

Where is the location of your light company?

_____

_____

Where is the location of your water and sewerage company?

_____

_____

Medical

Where is the location of your Urgent Care?

_____

_____

Where is the location of your family physician?

_____

_____

Where is the location of your family dentistry?

_____

_____

Education

Where is the location of the library?

_____
_____

Where is the location of the elementary school?

_____
_____

Where is the location of the middle school?

_____
_____

Where is the location of the high school?

_____
_____

Where is the location of the vocational school?

_____
_____

Where is the location of the community college?

_____
_____

Where is the location of the university?

_____
_____

Auto-Related Service

Where is the location of the gas station?

_____
_____

Where is the location of the auto service repair/dealership?

_____
_____

Where is the location of the rental car agency?

_____
_____

What is the name of your auto insurance, agent's name and contact information?

_____
_____

Entertainment/Leisure

Where is the location of the grocery store/shopping plaza?

_____
_____

Where is the location of your favorite restaurant(s)?

_____
_____

Where is the location of your barbershop/beauty shop/hairstylist?

_____
_____

Where is the location of the movie theater?

_____

_____

List the most popular landmarks in this community and why.

1. _____

_____

_____

2. _____

_____

_____

3. _____

_____

_____

4. _____

_____

_____

5. _____

_____

_____

CONNECTING DOT (1-D)

What does your picture look like in this area?

_____
_____
_____
_____
_____
_____
_____
_____
_____

What did you learn about yourself?

_____
_____
_____
_____
_____
_____
_____
_____
_____
_____

What, if any, steps will you begin to implement to draw a different picture to improve this area of your life?

HOMEOWNERSHIP: ORIGINAL MORTGAGE SIGNING

My original mortgage date is _____

My mortgage company is _____

The type of loan I possess is a _____

The advantages of possessing this type of loan are…

_____
_____
_____
_____

The disadvantages of possessing this type of loan are …

_____
_____
_____
_____

What were your thoughts/feelings during the closing of your first mortgage?

_____
_____
_____
_____

HOMEOWNERSHIP: ORIGINAL INTEREST RATE

My interest rate is _____

The advantages of this interest rate are …

_____

_____

_____

_____

_____

The disadvantages of this interest rate are …

_____

_____

_____

_____

_____

My original home loan was $ _____ .

My original mortgage principal was $ _____ .

My original mortgage interest that I would have paid at the end of my loan would have been $ _____ .

My original monthly mortgage payment is $ _____ .

My current amount in escrow is $ _____ .

HOMEOWNERSHIP: REFINANCE

What was the purpose of refinancing my home?

_____

_____

_____

_____

My refinance home loan is $ _____.

My refinance principal is $ _____.

The interest that I will have to pay now at the end of the refinance loan is $ _____.

My new monthly mortgage payment is $ _____.

My new interest rate is _____

The advantages of this new interest rate are …

_____

_____

_____

_____

The disadvantages of this new interest rate are …

_____

_____

_____

_____

My current amount in escrow is $ _____.

HOMEOWNERSHIP: INSURANCE

ACTION STEPS!

1. Locate your homeowner's insurance policy.
2. Read carefully your homeowner's insurance policy.
3. Highlight any discrepancies with the policy.
4. Immediately report those discrepancies to your insurance agent.
5. What additional coverage would you like to include in your current policy, e.g. flood insurance, etc.?

24 – MONTH MORTGAGE PAYMENT HISTORY

BEGINNING LOAN BALANCE $ _____

Preferably write in pencil.

Note: to get new ending balance, deduct current payment from previous ending balance.

$ _____   PAID ON _____   ENDING BALANCE $ _____

$ _____   PAID ON _____   ENDING BALANCE $ _____

$ _____   PAID ON _____   ENDING BALANCE $ _____

$ _____   PAID ON _____   ENDING BALANCE $ _____

$ _____   PAID ON _____   ENDING BALANCE $ _____

$ _____   PAID ON _____   ENDING BALANCE $ _____

$ _____   PAID ON _____   ENDING BALANCE $ _____

$ _____   PAID ON _____   ENDING BALANCE $ _____

$ _____   PAID ON _____   ENDING BALANCE $ _____

$ _____   PAID ON _____   ENDING BALANCE $ _____

$ _____   PAID ON _____   ENDING BALANCE $ _____

$ _____   PAID ON _____   ENDING BALANCE $ _____

$ _____   PAID ON _____   ENDING BALANCE $ _____

$ _____   PAID ON _____   ENDING BALANCE $ _____

$ _____   PAID ON _____   ENDING BALANCE $ _____

$ _____   PAID ON _____   ENDING BALANCE $ _____

$ _____   PAID ON _____   ENDING BALANCE $ _____

$ _____   PAID ON _____   ENDING BALANCE $ _____

$ _____   PAID ON _____   ENDING BALANCE $ _____

$ _____   PAID ON _____   ENDING BALANCE $ _____

$ _____   PAID ON _____   ENDING BALANCE $ _____

$ _____   PAID ON _____   ENDING BALANCE $ _____

$ _____   PAID ON _____   ENDING BALANCE $ _____

$ _____   PAID ON _____   ENDING BALANCE $ _____

ADDITIONAL NOTES

_____

_____

_____

_____

_____

_____

_____

_____

_____

_____

_____

_____

_____

_____

_____

_____

HOMEOWNERSHIP: HOME IMPROVEMENTS

DATE OF SERVICE	REASON FOR SERVICE	AMOUNT SPENT
		$
		$
		$
		$
		$
		$
		$
		$
		$
		$
		$
		$
		$
		$
		$
		$
		$
		$
		$
		$
		$

RENTAL

My rental manager/rental company/landlord is named:

_____

The office is located at _____

_____

My rent is due by _____

My rental payment is $ _____

I have been renting at my current address for _____ years or months.

I have invested approximately $ _____ as a renter.

The reason why I have not purchased a home yet is because:

_____

_____

_____

_____

ACTION STEPS!

1. Locate your renter's insurance policy.

2. Read carefully your renter's insurance policy.

3. Highlight any discrepancies with the policy.

4. Immediately report those discrepancies to your insurance agent.

5. What additional coverage would you like to include in your current policy?

24 –MONTH RENTAL PAYMENT HISTORY

MONTHLY RENTAL $ _____

Preferably write in pencil.

Note: to get total investment, add current rental payment to previous rental payment.

$ _____   PAID ON _____   TOTAL PAYMENT $ _____

$ _____   PAID ON _____   TOTAL PAYMENT $ _____

$ _____   PAID ON _____   TOTAL PAYMENT $ _____

$ _____   PAID ON _____   TOTAL PAYMENT $ _____

$ _____   PAID ON _____   TOTAL PAYMENT $ _____

$ _____   PAID ON _____   TOTAL PAYMENT $ _____

$ _____   PAID ON _____   TOTAL PAYMENT $ _____

$ _____   PAID ON _____   TOTAL PAYMENT $ _____

$ _____   PAID ON _____   TOTAL PAYMENT $ _____

$ _____   PAID ON _____   TOTAL PAYMENT $ _____

$ _____   PAID ON _____   TOTAL PAYMENT $ _____

$ _____   PAID ON _____   TOTAL PAYMENT $ _____

$ _____   PAID ON _____   TOTAL PAYMENT $ _____

$ _____   PAID ON _____   TOTAL PAYMENT $ _____

$ _____   PAID ON _____   TOTAL PAYMENT $ _____

$ _____   PAID ON _____   TOTAL PAYMENT $ _____

$ _____   PAID ON _____   TOTAL PAYMENT $ _____

$ _____   PAID ON _____   TOTAL PAYMENT $ _____

$ _____   PAID ON _____   TOTAL PAYMENT $ _____

$ _____   PAID ON _____   TOTAL PAYMENT $ _____

$ _____   PAID ON _____   TOTAL PAYMENT $ _____

$ _____   PAID ON _____   TOTAL PAYMENT $ _____

$ _____   PAID ON _____   TOTAL PAYMENT $ _____

$ _____   PAID ON _____   TOTAL PAYMENT $ _____

Grand total of investments at the end of 24 months $ _____

ADDITIONAL NOTES

_____

_____

_____

_____

_____

_____

_____

_____

_____

_____

_____

_____

_____

_____

CONNECTING DOTS (1E-1I)

What does your picture look like in this area?

What did you learn about yourself?

What, if any, steps will you begin to implement to draw a different picture to improve this area of your life?

DOT #2

FINANCES

MONEY IS NOT EVERYTHING BUT IT HELPS TO HAVE SOME

DOT #2-A   EMPLOYMENT: PAST AND PRESENT

DOT #2-B   ENTREPRENUERSHIP

DOT #2-C   BANKING:

                 ACCOUNTS, CHECKING, TRANSACTIONS, FACTORS AFFECTING BANKING SYSTEM

DOT #2-D   CREDIT:

                 CREDIT STATUS, CREDITORS, CREDIT CARDS, ACTIVE CREDITORS, CREDIT BUREAUS

DOT #2-E   EFFECTS OF BAD CREDIT:

                 JUDGEMENTS, FORECLOSURES, REPOSSESSIONS

DOT #2-F   PAYING BILLS

DOT #2-G   ASSETS

DOT #2-H   LIABILITIES

DOT #2-I   RETIREMENT

EMPLOYMENT: PAST

My previous place of employment was at _____

I was employed for _____ years/months.

My position/title was _____

I am no longer employed there because _____

_____

_____

My previous place of employment was _____

I was employed for _____ years/months.

My position/title was _____

The primary duties consisted of _____

I am no longer employed there because _____

_____

_____

My previous place of employment was _____

I was employed for _____ years/months.

My position/title was _____

The primary duties consisted of _____

I am no longer employed there because _____

_____

_____

My previous place of employment was _____

I was employed for _____ years/months.

My position/title was _____

The primary duties consisted of _____

I am no longer employed there because _____

_____

_____

My previous place of employment was _____

I was employed for _____ years/months.

My position/title was _____

The primary duties consisted of _____

I am no longer employed there because _____

_____

_____

My previous place of employment was _____

I was employed for _____ years/months.

My position/title was _____

The primary duties consisted of _____

I am no longer employed there because _____

_____

_____

Describe the first time you were terminated from a place of employment.

___

Describe the first (30) days following the termination of employment.

___

Describe the first (90) days following termination of employment.

___

Describe the circumstances on how you secured employment after this termination.

_____

_____

_____

_____

_____

_____

What would you have done differently to have avoided being terminated?

_____

_____

_____

_____

_____

_____

How has this termination, if any helped you to mature professionally?

_____

_____

_____

_____

_____

_____

Describe the second time you were terminated from a place of employment.

___

Describe the first (30) days following the termination of employment.

___

Describe the first (90) days following termination of employment.

___

Describe the circumstances on how you secured employment after this termination.

_____
_____
_____
_____
_____
_____

What would you have done differently to have avoided being terminated?

_____
_____
_____
_____
_____
_____

How has this termination, if any helped you to mature professionally?

_____
_____
_____
_____
_____
_____

Describe the third time you were terminated from a place of employment.

Describe the first (30) days following the termination of employment.

Describe the first (90) days following termination of employment.

Describe the circumstances on how you secured employment after this termination.

_____
_____
_____
_____
_____
_____

What would you have done differently to have avoided being terminated?

_____
_____
_____
_____
_____
_____

How has this termination, if any helped you to mature professionally?

_____
_____
_____
_____
_____
_____

Describe the first time you were laid-off from a place of employment.

_____
_____
_____
_____
_____
_____

Describe the first (30) days following the lay-off of employment.

_____
_____
_____
_____
_____
_____

Describe the first (90) days following lay-off of employment.

_____
_____
_____
_____
_____
_____

Describe the circumstances on how you secured employment after the lay-off.

What would you have done differently, if any to have avoided being laid-off?

How has this lay-off, if any helped you to mature professionally?

EMPLOYMENT: PRESENT

My current place of employment is _____

I have been employed for _____ years/months.

My professional degree(s) are …

1. _____
2. _____
3. _____

My professional licenses are …

1. _____
2. _____
3. _____

My professional certifications are …

1. _____
2. _____
3. _____

My vocational skills consist of …

1. _____
2. _____
3. _____

My work ethics consists of …

1. _____
2. _____
3. _____

I enjoy my current employment because …

1. _____
   _____

2. _____
   _____

3. _____
   _____

4. _____
   _____

I dislike my current employment because …

1. _____
   _____

2. _____
   _____

3. _____
   _____

4. _____
   _____

These are my job duties as outlined in my job description …

1. _____
2. _____
3. _____
4. _____
5. _____
6. _____
7. _____
8. _____
9. _____
10. _____

These are the duties that I perform that are not outlined in my job description …

1. _____
2. _____
3. _____
4. _____
5. _____
6. _____
7. _____
8. _____
9. _____
10. _____

Describe my working conditions.

_____
_____
_____
_____
_____
_____

Describe the working relationship with my supervisor.

_____
_____
_____
_____
_____
_____

Describe the working relationships with my co-workers.

_____
_____
_____
_____
_____
_____

Red Flags of my job (warnings)

1. _____
2. _____
3. _____
4. _____
5. _____
6. _____
7. _____

List a secondary career choice and why.

_____
_____
_____
_____
_____
_____
_____

List a third career choice and why.

_____
_____
_____
_____
_____
_____
_____

TRACKING MY EMPLOYMENT ATTENDANCE

ARRIVED AT:	WHO WAS PRESENT?	DEPARTED AT:	WHO WAS LEFT IN THE OFFICE?

ENTREPRENEURSHIP

I have been in business for _____ years/months.

My business is called _____

The reason why I chose this business name is …

_____

_____

_____

_____

My primary trade/sell is/are …

_____

_____

_____

_____

My secondary trade/sell is/are …

_____

_____

_____

_____

My primary customers are … and why?

_____

_____

_____

_____

What are the advantages of entrepreneurship?

The steps I can begin to implement to enhance my business ...

CONNECTING DOTS (2A-2B)

What does your picture look like in this area?

What did you learn about yourself?

What, if any, steps will you begin to implement to draw a different picture to improve this area of your life?

BANKING: ACCOUNTS

The primary purpose of a bank is ...

The primary purpose of a credit union is ...

The primary purpose of a checking account is ...

The primary purpose of a savings account is …

The primary purpose of a joint account is …

The primary purpose of a money market account is …

BANKING: CHECKING

What is a check?

_____

_____

_____

_____

_____

_____

_____

_____

What is meant by the term "routing number"?

_____

_____

_____

_____

_____

_____

_____

_____

What is meant by the term "account number"?

_____

_____

_____

_____

_____

_____

_____

_____

What is meant by the term "overdraft"?

What is meant by the acronym "NSF"?

What is the purpose of "Telecheck Recovery Systems"?

BANKING: TRANSACTIONS

What is a deposit?

What is a withdrawal?

What is a debit?

What is a pre-authorization debit?

What is payroll deduction?

What is the difference between a cashier's check and a money order?

FACTORS AFFECTING THE BANKING SYSTEM

What is the role of the Federal Reserves?

___

What is inflation?

___

Define interest rates.

___

What is a loan?

What is a share holder?

What are dividends?

What is the purpose of the stock market?

_____
_____
_____
_____
_____

List the full names of the three major stock markets in the United States.

1. _____
2. _____
3. _____

What is the purpose of an investment company?

_____
_____
_____
_____
_____

List three major investment companies.

1. _____
2. _____
3. _____

CHECKING ACCOUNT INFORMATION

Definitions:

Deposit/Credit = money that is added to the account, e.g. payroll check.

Withdrawal/Debit = money that is subtracted from the account, e.g., a purchase.

Ending Balance = money that remains after a withdrawal/debit has been processed.

Instructions for Checking Account Exercise:

1. Write the amount of money that you have spent on purchases and withdrawing money from your account in the (Withdrawal/Debit) column.

2. The amount of money that remains is your (Ending Balance) or what you have left. This amount is now considered a credit and will be transferred to the first column.

3. Continue these steps to ensure good record keeping and prevent overdrafts.

4. Preferably write in pencil.

CHECKING ACCOUNT HISTORY

DEPOSIT (+) CREDIT	WITHDRAWAL (-) DEBIT	ENDING BALANCE
$ _____	$ _____	$ _____
$ _____	$ _____	$ _____
$ _____	$ _____	$ _____
$ _____	$ _____	$ _____
$ _____	$ _____	$ _____
$ _____	$ _____	$ _____
$ _____	$ _____	$ _____
$ _____	$ _____	$ _____
$ _____	$ _____	$ _____
$ _____	$ _____	$ _____
$ _____	$ _____	$ _____
$ _____	$ _____	$ _____
$ _____	$ _____	$ _____
$ _____	$ _____	$ _____
$ _____	$ _____	$ _____
$ _____	$ _____	$ _____
$ _____	$ _____	$ _____
$ _____	$ _____	$ _____
$ _____	$ _____	$ _____
$ _____	$ _____	$ _____
$ _____	$ _____	$ _____

SAVINGS ACCOUNT INFORMATION

Definitions:

Deposit/Credit = money that is added to the account, e.g. payroll check.

Withdrawal/Debit = money that is subtracted from the account, e.g., a purchase.

Instructions for Savings Account Information:

1. Write the amount of money you currently have in your savings account that is above zero in the (Deposit/Credit) column.

2. Write the amount of money you that you have withdrew out of your account in the (Withdrawal/Debit) column.

3. The amount of money that remains is your (Ending Balance) or what you have left. This amount is now considered a credit and will be transferred to the first column.

4. Continue these steps to ensure good record keeping and prevent overdrafts.

5. Preferably write in pencil.

SAVINGS ACCOUNT HISTORY

DEPOSIT (+) CREDIT	WITHDRAWAL (-) DEBIT	ENDING BALANCE
$ _____	$ _____	$ _____
$ _____	$ _____	$ _____
$ _____	$ _____	$ _____
$ _____	$ _____	$ _____
$ _____	$ _____	$ _____
$ _____	$ _____	$ _____
$ _____	$ _____	$ _____
$ _____	$ _____	$ _____
$ _____	$ _____	$ _____
$ _____	$ _____	$ _____
$ _____	$ _____	$ _____
$ _____	$ _____	$ _____
$ _____	$ _____	$ _____
$ _____	$ _____	$ _____
$ _____	$ _____	$ _____
$ _____	$ _____	$ _____
$ _____	$ _____	$ _____
$ _____	$ _____	$ _____
$ _____	$ _____	$ _____
$ _____	$ _____	$ _____
$ _____	$ _____	$ _____
$ _____	$ _____	$ _____

CONNECTING DOT (2-C)

What does your picture look like in this area?

_____
_____
_____
_____
_____
_____
_____
_____
_____
_____

What did you learn about yourself?

_____
_____
_____
_____
_____
_____
_____
_____
_____
_____
_____
_____

What, if any, steps will you begin to implement to draw a different picture to improve this area of your life?

CREDIT: STATUS

What is credit?

_____

_____

_____

_____

_____

_____

_____

What is a "credit score"?

_____

_____

_____

_____

_____

_____

What is meant by the term "good credit"? What is meant by the term "bad credit"?

_____

_____

_____

_____

_____

CREDIT: CREDITORS

What is meant by the word "creditor"?

What is the primary purpose of a "finance company"?

What is meant by the term "to finance"?

What is meant by the term "finance charge"?

What is meant by the term "interest rate"?

What is meant by the term "Predatory Lending"?

List three companies that you have experienced or became aware of that promote "Predatory Lending". Describe their company policies and discuss their interest rates.

Describe how you were able to overcome the vicious cycle of "Predatory Lending".

CREDIT: CREDIT CARDS

What is a credit card?

_____
_____
_____
_____

What is an "unsecured" credit card?

_____
_____
_____
_____

What is a "secured" credit card"?

_____
_____
_____
_____

What is a "pre-paid debit" card?

_____
_____
_____
_____

What is meant by the term "pre-approved"?

What is meant by the term "annual percentage rate" (APR)?

What is meant by the term "variable rate"?

What is meant by the term "credit limit"?

What is meant by the term "available credit"?

What is meant by the term "pay the minimum amount"?

CREDIT CARDS

The name of my credit card is _____

This credit card is funded by _____

My original line of credit was for $ _____

My annual percentage rate (APR) is $ _____

My annual fee is $ _____

My monthly payment is $ _____

My outstanding balance is $ _____

The name of my credit card is _____

This credit card is funded by _____

My original line of credit was for $ _____

My annual percentage rate (APR) is $ _____

My annual fee is $ _____

My monthly payment is $ _____

My outstanding balance is $ _____

The name of my credit card is _____

This credit card is funded by _____

My original line of credit was for $ _____

My annual percentage rate (APR) is $ _____

My annual fee is $ _____

My monthly payment is $ _____

My outstanding balance is $ _____

MONTHLY PAYMENT HISTORY

FOR MY _____ CREDIT CARD

$ _____ PAID ON _____   ENDING BALANCE $ _____

$ _____ PAID ON _____   ENDING BALANCE $ _____

$ _____ PAID ON _____   ENDING BALANCE $ _____

$ _____ PAID ON _____   ENDING BALANCE $ _____

$ _____ PAID ON _____   ENDING BALANCE $ _____

$ _____ PAID ON _____   ENDING BALANCE $ _____

$ _____ PAID ON _____   ENDING BALANCE $ _____

$ _____ PAID ON _____   ENDING BALANCE $ _____

$ _____ PAID ON _____   ENDING BALANCE $ _____

$ _____ PAID ON _____   ENDING BALANCE $ _____

$ _____ PAID ON _____   ENDING BALANCE $ _____

$ _____ PAID ON _____   ENDING BALANCE $ _____

$ _____ PAID ON _____   ENDING BALANCE $ _____

$ _____ PAID ON _____   ENDING BALANCE $ _____

$ _____ PAID ON _____   ENDING BALANCE $ _____

$ _____ PAID ON _____   ENDING BALANCE $ _____

$ _____ PAID ON _____   ENDING BALANCE $ _____

$ _____ PAID ON _____   ENDING BALANCE $ _____

$ _____ PAID ON _____   ENDING BALANCE $ _____

$ _____ PAID ON _____   ENDING BALANCE $ _____

$ _____ PAID ON _____   ENDING BALANCE $ _____

MONTHLY PAYMENT HISTORY

<u>FOR MY</u> _____ <u>CREDIT CARD</u>

$ _____ PAID ON _____   ENDING BALANCE $ _____

$ _____ PAID ON _____   ENDING BALANCE $ _____

$ _____ PAID ON _____   ENDING BALANCE $ _____

$ _____ PAID ON _____   ENDING BALANCE $ _____

$ _____ PAID ON _____   ENDING BALANCE $ _____

$ _____ PAID ON _____   ENDING BALANCE $ _____

$ _____ PAID ON _____   ENDING BALANCE $ _____

$ _____ PAID ON _____   ENDING BALANCE $ _____

$ _____ PAID ON _____   ENDING BALANCE $ _____

$ _____ PAID ON _____   ENDING BALANCE $ _____

$ _____ PAID ON _____   ENDING BALANCE $ _____

$ _____ PAID ON _____   ENDING BALANCE $ _____

$ _____ PAID ON _____   ENDING BALANCE $ _____

$ _____ PAID ON _____   ENDING BALANCE $ _____

$ _____ PAID ON _____   ENDING BALANCE $ _____

$ _____ PAID ON _____   ENDING BALANCE $ _____

$ _____ PAID ON _____   ENDING BALANCE $ _____

$ _____ PAID ON _____   ENDING BALANCE $ _____

$ _____ PAID ON _____   ENDING BALANCE $ _____

$ _____ PAID ON _____   ENDING BALANCE $ _____

$ _____ PAID ON _____   ENDING BALANCE $ _____

MONTHLY PAYMENT HISTORY

<u>FOR MY</u> _____ <u>CREDIT CARD</u>

$ _____ PAID ON _____ ENDING BALANCE $ _____

$ _____ PAID ON _____ ENDING BALANCE $ _____

$ _____ PAID ON _____ ENDING BALANCE $ _____

$ _____ PAID ON _____ ENDING BALANCE $ _____

$ _____ PAID ON _____ ENDING BALANCE $ _____

$ _____ PAID ON _____ ENDING BALANCE $ _____

$ _____ PAID ON _____ ENDING BALANCE $ _____

$ _____ PAID ON _____ ENDING BALANCE $ _____

$ _____ PAID ON _____ ENDING BALANCE $ _____

$ _____ PAID ON _____ ENDING BALANCE $ _____

$ _____ PAID ON _____ ENDING BALANCE $ _____

$ _____ PAID ON _____ ENDING BALANCE $ _____

$ _____ PAID ON _____ ENDING BALANCE $ _____

$ _____ PAID ON _____ ENDING BALANCE $ _____

$ _____ PAID ON _____ ENDING BALANCE $ _____

$ _____ PAID ON _____ ENDING BALANCE $ _____

$ _____ PAID ON _____ ENDING BALANCE $ _____

$ _____ PAID ON _____ ENDING BALANCE $ _____

$ _____ PAID ON _____ ENDING BALANCE $ _____

$ _____ PAID ON _____ ENDING BALANCE $ _____

ACTIVE CREDITORS

(Non-credit cards)

My creditor is _____

The location is _____

The contact # is _____

Web Address is _____

My outstanding balance is $ _____

My monthly payment is $ _____

My creditor is _____

The location is _____

The contact # is _____

Web Address is _____

My outstanding balance is $ _____

My monthly payment is $ _____

My creditor is _____

The location is _____

The contact # is _____

Web Address is _____

My outstanding balance is $_____

My monthly payment is $ _____

ACTIVE CREDITORS

(Non-credit cards)

My creditor is _____

The location is _____

The contact # is _____

Web Address is _____

My outstanding balance is $ _____

My monthly payment is $ _____

My creditor is _____

The location is _____

The contact # is _____

Web Address is _____

My outstanding balance is $ _____

My monthly payment is $ _____

My creditor is _____

The location is _____

The contact # is _____

Web Address is _____

My outstanding balance is $_____

My monthly payment is $ _____

MONTHLY PAYMENT HISTORY

FOR MY ACTIVE CREDITOR _____

$ _____ PAID ON _____ ENDING BALANCE $ _____

$ _____ PAID ON _____ ENDING BALANCE $ _____

$ _____ PAID ON _____ ENDING BALANCE $ _____

$ _____ PAID ON _____ ENDING BALANCE $ _____

$ _____ PAID ON _____ ENDING BALANCE $ _____

$ _____ PAID ON _____ ENDING BALANCE $ _____

$ _____ PAID ON _____ ENDING BALANCE $ _____

$ _____ PAID ON _____ ENDING BALANCE $ _____

$ _____ PAID ON _____ ENDING BALANCE $ _____

$ _____ PAID ON _____ ENDING BALANCE $ _____

$ _____ PAID ON _____ ENDING BALANCE $ _____

$ _____ PAID ON _____ ENDING BALANCE $ _____

$ _____ PAID ON _____ ENDING BALANCE $ _____

$ _____ PAID ON _____ ENDING BALANCE $ _____

$ _____ PAID ON _____ ENDING BALANCE $ _____

$ _____ PAID ON _____ ENDING BALANCE $ _____

$ _____ PAID ON _____ ENDING BALANCE $ _____

$ _____ PAID ON _____ ENDING BALANCE $ _____

$ _____ PAID ON _____ ENDING BALANCE $ _____

$ _____ PAID ON _____ ENDING BALANCE $ _____

$ _____ PAID ON _____ ENDING BALANCE $ _____

MONTHLY PAYMENT HISTORY

FOR MY ACTIVE CREDITOR _____

$ _____	PAID ON _____	ENDING BALANCE	$ _____
$ _____	PAID ON _____	ENDING BALANCE	$ _____
$ _____	PAID ON _____	ENDING BALANCE	$ _____
$ _____	PAID ON _____	ENDING BALANCE	$ _____
$ _____	PAID ON _____	ENDING BALANCE	$ _____
$ _____	PAID ON _____	ENDING BALANCE	$ _____
$ _____	PAID ON _____	ENDING BALANCE	$ _____
$ _____	PAID ON _____	ENDING BALANCE	$ _____
$ _____	PAID ON _____	ENDING BALANCE	$ _____
$ _____	PAID ON _____	ENDING BALANCE	$ _____
$ _____	PAID ON _____	ENDING BALANCE	$ _____
$ _____	PAID ON _____	ENDING BALANCE	$ _____
$ _____	PAID ON _____	ENDING BALANCE	$ _____
$ _____	PAID ON _____	ENDING BALANCE	$ _____
$ _____	PAID ON _____	ENDING BALANCE	$ _____
$ _____	PAID ON _____	ENDING BALANCE	$ _____
$ _____	PAID ON _____	ENDING BALANCE	$ _____
$ _____	PAID ON _____	ENDING BALANCE	$ _____
$ _____	PAID ON _____	ENDING BALANCE	$ _____
$ _____	PAID ON _____	ENDING BALANCE	$ _____
$ _____	PAID ON _____	ENDING BALANCE	$ _____

MONTHLY PAYMENT HISTORY

<u>FOR MY ACTIVE CREDITOR</u> _____

$ _____   PAID ON _____   ENDING BALANCE $ _____

$ _____   PAID ON _____   ENDING BALANCE $ _____

$ _____   PAID ON _____   ENDING BALANCE $ _____

$ _____   PAID ON _____   ENDING BALANCE $ _____

$ _____   PAID ON _____   ENDING BALANCE $ _____

$ _____   PAID ON _____   ENDING BALANCE $ _____

$ _____   PAID ON _____   ENDING BALANCE $ _____

$ _____   PAID ON _____   ENDING BALANCE $ _____

$ _____   PAID ON _____   ENDING BALANCE $ _____

$ _____   PAID ON _____   ENDING BALANCE $ _____

$ _____   PAID ON _____   ENDING BALANCE $ _____

$ _____   PAID ON _____   ENDING BALANCE $ _____

$ _____   PAID ON _____   ENDING BALANCE $ _____

$ _____   PAID ON _____   ENDING BALANCE $ _____

$ _____   PAID ON _____   ENDING BALANCE $ _____

$ _____   PAID ON _____   ENDING BALANCE $ _____

$ _____   PAID ON _____   ENDING BALANCE $ _____

$ _____   PAID ON _____   ENDING BALANCE $ _____

$ _____   PAID ON _____   ENDING BALANCE $ _____

$ _____   PAID ON _____   ENDING BALANCE $ _____

MONTHLY PAYMENT HISTORY

<u>FOR MY ACTIVE CREDITOR</u> _____

$ _____ PAID ON _____ ENDING BALANCE $ _____

$ _____ PAID ON _____ ENDING BALANCE $ _____

$ _____ PAID ON _____ ENDING BALANCE $ _____

$ _____ PAID ON _____ ENDING BALANCE $ _____

$ _____ PAID ON _____ ENDING BALANCE $ _____

$ _____ PAID ON _____ ENDING BALANCE $ _____

$ _____ PAID ON _____ ENDING BALANCE $ _____

$ _____ PAID ON _____ ENDING BALANCE $ _____

$ _____ PAID ON _____ ENDING BALANCE $ _____

$ _____ PAID ON _____ ENDING BALANCE $ _____

$ _____ PAID ON _____ ENDING BALANCE $ _____

$ _____ PAID ON _____ ENDING BALANCE $ _____

$ _____ PAID ON _____ ENDING BALANCE $ _____

$ _____ PAID ON _____ ENDING BALANCE $ _____

$ _____ PAID ON _____ ENDING BALANCE $ _____

$ _____ PAID ON _____ ENDING BALANCE $ _____

$ _____ PAID ON _____ ENDING BALANCE $ _____

$ _____ PAID ON _____ ENDING BALANCE $ _____

$ _____ PAID ON _____ ENDING BALANCE $ _____

$ _____ PAID ON _____ ENDING BALANCE $ _____

$ _____ PAID ON _____ ENDING BALANCE $ _____

MONTHLY PAYMENT HISTORY

<u>FOR MY ACTIVE CREDITOR</u> _____

$ _____	PAID ON _____	ENDING BALANCE	$ _____
$ _____	PAID ON _____	ENDING BALANCE	$ _____
$ _____	PAID ON _____	ENDING BALANCE	$ _____
$ _____	PAID ON _____	ENDING BALANCE	$ _____
$ _____	PAID ON _____	ENDING BALANCE	$ _____
$ _____	PAID ON _____	ENDING BALANCE	$ _____
$ _____	PAID ON _____	ENDING BALANCE	$ _____
$ _____	PAID ON _____	ENDING BALANCE	$ _____
$ _____	PAID ON _____	ENDING BALANCE	$ _____
$ _____	PAID ON _____	ENDING BALANCE	$ _____
$ _____	PAID ON _____	ENDING BALANCE	$ _____
$ _____	PAID ON _____	ENDING BALANCE	$ _____
$ _____	PAID ON _____	ENDING BALANCE	$ _____
$ _____	PAID ON _____	ENDING BALANCE	$ _____
$ _____	PAID ON _____	ENDING BALANCE	$ _____
$ _____	PAID ON _____	ENDING BALANCE	$ _____
$ _____	PAID ON _____	ENDING BALANCE	$ _____
$ _____	PAID ON _____	ENDING BALANCE	$ _____
$ _____	PAID ON _____	ENDING BALANCE	$ _____
$ _____	PAID ON _____	ENDING BALANCE	$ _____
$ _____	PAID ON _____	ENDING BALANCE	$ _____

MONTHLY PAYMENT HISTORY

FOR MY ACTIVE CREDITOR _____

$ _____   PAID ON _____   ENDING BALANCE $ _____

$ _____   PAID ON _____   ENDING BALANCE $ _____

$ _____   PAID ON _____   ENDING BALANCE $ _____

$ _____   PAID ON _____   ENDING BALANCE $ _____

$ _____   PAID ON _____   ENDING BALANCE $ _____

$ _____   PAID ON _____   ENDING BALANCE $ _____

$ _____   PAID ON _____   ENDING BALANCE $ _____

$ _____   PAID ON _____   ENDING BALANCE $ _____

$ _____   PAID ON _____   ENDING BALANCE $ _____

$ _____   PAID ON _____   ENDING BALANCE $ _____

$ _____   PAID ON _____   ENDING BALANCE $ _____

$ _____   PAID ON _____   ENDING BALANCE $ _____

$ _____   PAID ON _____   ENDING BALANCE $ _____

$ _____   PAID ON _____   ENDING BALANCE $ _____

$ _____   PAID ON _____   ENDING BALANCE $ _____

$ _____   PAID ON _____   ENDING BALANCE $ _____

$ _____   PAID ON _____   ENDING BALANCE $ _____

$ _____   PAID ON _____   ENDING BALANCE $ _____

$ _____   PAID ON _____   ENDING BALANCE $ _____

$ _____   PAID ON _____   ENDING BALANCE $ _____

$ _____   PAID ON _____   ENDING BALANCE $ _____

CREDIT BUREAUS

What is the purpose of the credit bureaus?

_____

_____

_____

_____

_____

_____

The three major credit bureaus are….

Credit bureau _____

The location is _____

Web Address is _____

The contact # is _____

Credit bureau _____

The location is _____

Web Address is _____

The contact # is _____

Credit bureau _____

The location is _____

Web Address is _____

The contact # is _____

CREDIT REPORT - ACTION STEPS!

1. Request your credit report from all three credit bureaus.

2. Read your credit report carefully.

3. If the credit report is accurate, proceed to the next section. If there are some discrepancies in the credit report, please continue with steps 4-10.

4. Highlight any creditors that you have paid-off or settled with that continues to show any accounts as delinquent.

5. Retrieve the receipts of the accounts.

6. Make copies of the receipts.

7. Write a letter to each credit bureau that continues to list those accounts as delinquent (include your full name, address and contact number).

8. Make a copy of the letter for your records.

9. Mail the letter and copies of the receipts to the credit bureaus.

10. Call the credit bureaus to dispute each account and inform them of your mailed letter (specify the date in which the letter was mailed).

11. Place a follow-up phone call to the credit bureaus two weeks after the letter was mailed.

CONNECTING DOT (2-D)

What does your picture look like in this area?

_____
_____
_____
_____
_____
_____
_____
_____
_____
_____

What did you learn about yourself?

_____
_____
_____
_____
_____
_____
_____
_____
_____
_____

What, if any, steps will you begin to implement to draw a different picture to improve this area of your life?

(2-E) EFFECTS OF BAD CREDIT

BANKRUPTCY

What is bankruptcy?

_____
_____
_____
_____
_____

Why would you consider filing bankruptcy?

_____
_____
_____
_____
_____

If you have filed bankruptcy, what factors contributed to this action?

_____
_____
_____
_____

What is the primary purpose of a bankruptcy attorney?

_____
_____
_____

ACTION STEPS!

1. Locate your Bankruptcy Discharge documentation.

2. Read each line carefully.

3. Count the number of years from the date of filing - calculating discharge date.

4. Make a list of the creditor(s) that were filed with the bankruptcy.

5. Compare the bankruptcy documents to your recent credit report.

6. Make a list of the creditors that continues to show delinquent on your credit report.

7. Contact these creditors and inform them that their accounts were listed on the bankruptcy.

8. Provide proof that their accounts were listed on the bankruptcy via mail or fax.

9. Write a letter to each credit bureau that continues to list those accounts as delinquent (include your full name, address and contact number).

10. Make a copy of the letter for your records.

11. Mail the letter and proof of the account listed on the bankruptcy to the credit bureaus.

12. Contact the credit bureaus to dispute each account and inform them of your mailed letter (specify the date when the letter was mailed).

13. Place a follow-up phone call to the credit bureaus two weeks after the letter is mailed.

JUDGMENTS

List the judgments and what occurred for you to receive these judgments.

JUDGMENT #1

_____

_____

JUDGMENT #2

_____

_____

JUDGMENT #3

_____

_____

JUDGMENT #4

_____

_____

JUDGMENT #5

_____

_____

FORECLOSURES

List the foreclosures and what occurred for you to have surrendered your homes..

_____

_____

_____

_____

_____

_____

REPOSSESSIONS

List the vehicle repossessions and what occurred for you to have surrendered your vehicles.

_____

_____

_____

_____

_____

_____

CONNECTING DOT (2-E)

What does your picture look like in this area?

_____
_____
_____
_____
_____
_____
_____
_____
_____
_____

What did you learn about yourself?

_____
_____
_____
_____
_____
_____
_____
_____
_____
_____
_____
_____

What, if any, steps will you begin to implement to draw a different picture to improve this area of your life?

(2-F) PAYING BILLS

What are/were your paternal grandfather's views on paying bills?
_____
_____
_____
_____

What are/were your paternal grandmother's views on paying bills?
_____
_____
_____
_____

What are/were your maternal grandfather's views on paying bills?
_____
_____
_____
_____

What are/were your maternal grandmother's views on paying bills?
_____
_____
_____
_____

What are/were your father's views on paying bills?

What are/were your mother's views on paying bills?

What are your views on paying bills?

WHAT ARE YOUR CURRENT BILLS AND STATUS OF PAYMENT?

CURRENT – WITHIN 30 DAYS
LATE - AFTER 30 DAYS
PAST DUE - MORE THAN 60 DAYS)

1. _____
2. _____
3. _____
4. _____
5. _____
6. _____
7. _____
8. _____
9. _____
10. _____
11. _____
12. _____
13. _____
14. _____
15. _____
16. _____
17. _____
18. _____
19. _____
20. _____

PRIORITIZE YOUR BILLS AND WHY?

1. _____
   _____

2. _____
   _____

3. _____
   _____

4. _____
   _____

5. _____
   _____

6. _____
   _____

7. _____
   _____

8. _____
   _____

9. _____
   _____

CONNECTING DOT (2-F)

What does your picture look like in this area?

What did you learn about yourself?

What, if any, steps will you begin to implement to draw a different picture to improve this area of your life?

(2-G) ASSETS

What are/were your paternal grandfather's assets?

_____
_____
_____
_____

What are/were your paternal grandmother's assets?

_____
_____
_____
_____

What are/were your maternal grandfather's assets?

_____
_____
_____
_____

What are/were your maternal grandmother's assets?

_____
_____
_____
_____

What are/were your father's assets?

_____
_____
_____
_____
_____

What are/were your mother's assets?

_____
_____
_____
_____
_____

What are your assets?

1. _____
2. _____
3. _____
4. _____
5. _____
6. _____
7. _____
8. _____
9. _____
10. _____

(2-H) LIABILITIES

What are/were your paternal grandfather's liabilities?

___

What are/were your paternal grandmother's liabilities?

___

What are/were your maternal grandfather's liabilities?

___

What are/were your maternal grandmother's liabilities?

___

What are/were your father's liabilities?

_____
_____
_____
_____

What are/were your mother's liabilities?

_____
_____
_____
_____

What are your liabilities?

1. _____
2. _____
3. _____
4. _____
5. _____
6. _____
7. _____
8. _____
9. _____
10. _____

CONNECTING DOTS (2G-2H)

What does your picture look like in this area?

What did you learn about yourself?

What, if any, steps will you begin to implement to draw a different picture to improve this area of your life?

(2-I) RETIREMENT

SOCIAL SECURITY

The social security office in my area is located at

_____

What is the purpose of social security benefits?

_____

_____

_____

List the years, length of time, and names of taxable employment – (employment that deducted social security benefits from my wages)

1. _____
2. _____
3. _____
4. _____
5. _____
6. _____
7. _____
8. _____
9. _____
10. _____

ACTION STEPS!

1. Read your social security statement carefully.

2. Highlight any discrepancies with your statement.

3. Write a brief statement regarding the discrepancy.

4. Visit your local social security administration building and speak to a representative and submit your written statement.

RETIREMENT PLANS

THE TYPE OF RETIREMENT PLAN I HAVE IS…

401k   _____
401b   _____
TSA   _____
OTHER   _____

I HAVE SELECTED THIS RETIREMENT PLAN BECAUSE

1. _____

   _____

2. _____

   _____

MY RETIREMENT PLAN PAYMENT IS $ _____

MONTHLY PAYMENT HISTORY

FOR RETIREMENT PLAN _____

$ _____	PAID ON _____	ENDING BALANCE	$ _____
$ _____	PAID ON _____	ENDING BALANCE	$ _____
$ _____	PAID ON _____	ENDING BALANCE	$ _____
$ _____	PAID ON _____	ENDING BALANCE	$ _____
$ _____	PAID ON _____	ENDING BALANCE	$ _____
$ _____	PAID ON _____	ENDING BALANCE	$ _____
$ _____	PAID ON _____	ENDING BALANCE	$ _____
$ _____	PAID ON _____	ENDING BALANCE	$ _____
$ _____	PAID ON _____	ENDING BALANCE	$ _____
$ _____	PAID ON _____	ENDING BALANCE	$ _____
$ _____	PAID ON _____	ENDING BALANCE	$ _____
$ _____	PAID ON _____	ENDING BALANCE	$ _____
$ _____	PAID ON _____	ENDING BALANCE	$ _____
$ _____	PAID ON _____	ENDING BALANCE	$ _____
$ _____	PAID ON _____	ENDING BALANCE	$ _____
$ _____	PAID ON _____	ENDING BALANCE	$ _____
$ _____	PAID ON _____	ENDING BALANCE	$ _____
$ _____	PAID ON _____	ENDING BALANCE	$ _____
$ _____	PAID ON _____	ENDING BALANCE	$ _____
$ _____	PAID ON _____	ENDING BALANCE	$ _____
$ _____	PAID ON _____	ENDING BALANCE	$ _____

IF I DON'T HAVE A RETIREMENT PLAN, THEN THESE ARE THE STEPS I NEED TO DO TO OBTAIN ONE?

1. _____
   _____

2. _____
   _____

3. _____
   _____

INVESTMENTS

My financial planner/advisor is _____

The name of my stock/mutual fund is _____

I have invested in this stock/mutual fund since _____

I have received $ _____ since my investment date.

As of today, my stock/mutual fund is worth _____

I can possibly yield a higher return by_____

My financial planner/advisor is _____

The name of my stock/mutual fund is _____

I have invested in this stock/mutual fund since _____

I have received $ _____ since my investment date.

As of today, my stock/mutual fund is worth _____

I can possibly yield a higher return by_____

My financial planner/advisor is _____

The name of my stock/mutual fund is _____

I have invested in this stock/mutual fund since _____

I have received $ _____ since my investment date.

As of today, my stock/mutual fund is worth _____

I can possibly yield a higher return by_____

CONNECTING DOT (2-I)

What does your picture look like in this area?

What did you learn about yourself?

What, if any, steps will you begin to implement to draw a different picture to improve this area of your life?

DOT #3

TRANSPORTATION - KEEPS YOU MOVING

DOT #3-A   EARLIEST MEMORIES

DOT #3-B   DRIVER'S LICENSE

DOT #3-C   HISTORY OF VEHICLE POSSESSION

DOT #3-D   THE NEED FOR TRANSPORTATION

DOT #3-E   AUTO FINANCE

DOT #3-F   TRANSPORTATION SERVICE NEEDS

(3-A) EARLIEST MEMORIES

What was your earliest memory of skating?

_____

_____

_____

_____

What was your earliest memory of skate boarding?

_____

_____

_____

_____

What was your earliest memory of riding a bicycle?

_____

_____

_____

_____

What was your earliest memory of riding the Yellow School Bus?

_____

_____

_____

_____

What was your earliest memory of riding Public Bus Transportation?

_____
_____
_____
_____

What was your earliest memory of riding the subway/public transit?

_____
_____
_____
_____

What was your earliest memory of riding in a cab?

_____
_____
_____
_____

What was your earliest memory of riding a train?

_____
_____
_____
_____

What was your earliest memory of riding on a plane?

_____
_____
_____
_____

(3-B) DRIVER'S LICENSE

What was your earliest memory of learning how to drive a motor vehicle prior to you participating in Driver's Education? Include who, what, when and where.

_____

_____

_____

_____

_____

What was your scariest memory of participating in Driver's Education?

_____

_____

_____

_____

_____

Describe your Road Test experience at the Secretary of State or Department Motor Vehicle including month, year, city/town, state/province, weather condition, time of day, duration of the road test, type of vehicle you operated, and who allowed you access to the vehicle:

_____

_____

_____

_____

_____

_____

CONNECTING DOTS (3A-3B)

What does your picture look like in this area?

_____
_____
_____
_____
_____
_____
_____
_____
_____
_____

What did you learn about yourself?

_____
_____
_____
_____
_____
_____
_____
_____
_____
_____
_____

What, if any, steps will you begin to implement to draw a different picture to improve this area of your life?

(3-C) HISTORY OF VEHICLE POSSESSIONS

What was the first vehicle you owned including year, make, model, color, how did you come into possession of it and duration of time with the vehicle?

_____
_____
_____
_____
_____

Describe a memorable event with this vehicle.

_____
_____
_____
_____
_____

Describe a least memorable event with this vehicle.

_____
_____
_____
_____

What ever happened to this vehicle?

_____
_____
_____
_____
_____

What was the second vehicle you owned including year, make, model, color, how did you come into possession of it and duration of time with the vehicle?

_____

_____

_____

_____

Describe a memorable event with this vehicle.

_____

_____

_____

_____

Describe a least memorable event with this vehicle.

_____

_____

_____

What ever happened to this vehicle?

_____

_____

_____

What was the third vehicle you owned including year, make, model, color, how did you come into possession of it and duration of time with the vehicle?

Describe a memorable event with this vehicle.

Describe a least memorable event with this vehicle.

What ever happened to this vehicle?

What was the fourth vehicle you owned including year, make, model, color, how did you come into possession of it and duration of time with the vehicle?

_____
_____
_____
_____
_____

Describe a memorable event with this vehicle.

_____
_____
_____
_____
_____

Describe a least memorable event with this vehicle.

_____
_____
_____
_____

What ever happened to this vehicle?

_____
_____
_____
_____

CONNECTING DOT (3-C)

What does your picture look like in this area?

_____
_____
_____
_____
_____
_____
_____
_____
_____

What did you learn about yourself?

_____
_____
_____
_____
_____
_____
_____
_____
_____
_____

What, if any, steps will you begin to implement to draw a different picture to improve this area of your life?

(3-D) THE NEED FOR TRANSPORTATION

Describe an experience that your vehicle was not operable yet you had an emergency.

_____
_____
_____
_____

Describe an experience that you depended upon someone to pick you up and they were late or never arrived.

_____
_____
_____
_____

Describe an experience that you either lost your keys or accidentally locked your keys in your vehicle.

_____
_____
_____
_____

Describe an experience that your vehicle was stolen or repossessed.

_____
_____
_____
_____

(3-E) **AUTO FINANCE**

The name/location/phone number/web address of the dealership in which I had purchased my vehicle:

_____

_____

_____

The name/location/phone number of the finance company which "financed" (loaned) me the money for my vehicle:

_____

_____

_____

I was originally approved for $_____ based upon my credit.

When you add my original approved loan amount plus the interest rate from the finance company, the total amount of my auto loan at signing was $ _____

This loan has to be re-paid in full within _____
                                                             (# of months)

My monthly payment is $ _____

My outstanding balance is the amount of money that remains after I make a monthly payment.

As of _____ my outstanding balance is $ _____
     (Today's date)

The name/location/phone number/web address of the dealership in which I had purchased my secondary vehicle:

_____
_____
_____

The name/location/phone number of the finance company which "financed" (loaned) me the money for my vehicle:

_____
_____
_____

I was originally approved for $_____ based upon my credit.

When you add my original approved loan amount plus the interest rate from the finance company, the total amount of my auto loan at signing was $ _____

This loan has to be re-paid in full within _____
                                                              (# of months)

My monthly payment is $ _____

My outstanding balance is the amount of money that remains after I make a monthly payment.

As of _____ my outstanding balance is $ _____
    (Today's date)

The name/location/phone number/web address of the dealership in which I had purchased my <u>third</u> vehicle:

_____

_____

_____

The name/location/phone number of the finance company which "financed" (loaned) me the money for my vehicle:

_____

_____

_____

I was originally approved for $_____ based upon my credit.

When you add my original approved loan amount plus the interest rate from the finance company, the total amount of my auto loan at signing was $ _____

This loan has to be re-paid in full within _____
                                                                            (# of months)

My monthly payment is $ _____

My outstanding balance is the amount of money that remains after I make a monthly payment.

As of _____ my outstanding balance is $ _____
      (Today's date)

List five of your "dream vehicles" of all time and why? Include the year, make, model, color – exterior and interior and any special features.

(3-F) TRANSPORTATION SERVICE NEEDS

DATE OF SERVICE	REASON FOR SERVICE	AMOUNT SPENT
		$
		$
		$
		$
		$
		$
		$
		$
		$
		$
		$
		$
		$

CONNECTING THE DOTS (3D-3F)

What does your picture look like in this area?

___

What did you learn about yourself?

___

What, if any, steps will you begin to implement to draw a different picture to improve this area of your life?

MONTHLY AUTO PAYMENT HISTORY

For Auto Finance Company

_____

Current Balance: $ _____

$ _____	PAID ON _____	ENDING BALANCE	$ _____
$ _____	PAID ON _____	ENDING BALANCE	$ _____
$ _____	PAID ON _____	ENDING BALANCE	$ _____
$ _____	PAID ON _____	ENDING BALANCE	$ _____
$ _____	PAID ON _____	ENDING BALANCE	$ _____
$ _____	PAID ON _____	ENDING BALANCE	$ _____
$ _____	PAID ON _____	ENDING BALANCE	$ _____
$ _____	PAID ON _____	ENDING BALANCE	$ _____
$ _____	PAID ON _____	ENDING BALANCE	$ _____
$ _____	PAID ON _____	ENDING BALANCE	$ _____
$ _____	PAID ON _____	ENDING BALANCE	$ _____
$ _____	PAID ON _____	ENDING BALANCE	$ _____
$ _____	PAID ON _____	ENDING BALANCE	$ _____
$ _____	PAID ON _____	ENDING BALANCE	$ _____
$ _____	PAID ON _____	ENDING BALANCE	$ _____
$ _____	PAID ON _____	ENDING BALANCE	$ _____
$ _____	PAID ON _____	ENDING BALANCE	$ _____
$ _____	PAID ON _____	ENDING BALANCE	$ _____
$ _____	PAID ON _____	ENDING BALANCE	$ _____
$ _____	PAID ON _____	ENDING BALANCE	$ _____

DOT #4

LEGAL

YOU CAN'T LIVE IF YOU ARE CONSTANTLY RUNNING

DOT #4-A   LEGITIMATE/PROBATION/PAROLE

DOT #4-B   COURT FEES and RESTITUTION

DOT #4-C   DRIVER'S LICENSE

DOT #4-D   UNPAID MOTOR VEHICLE TICKETS (MOVING OR PARKED)

DOT #4-E   OUTSTANDING INCOME TAXES

DOT #4-F   PROPERTY TAXES

DOT #4-G   CHILD SUPPORT

DOT #4-H   ALIMONY

DOT #4-I   HUMAN SERVICES

(4-A) LEGITIMATE
LEGAL STATUS

My current legal status is _____

If my response is anything other than **legitimate**, I should complete the following…

PROBATION/PAROLE OFFICER

My probation/parole officer is _____

The location is _____

The contact numbers are _____

My probation/parole officer's e-mail is _____

My report date and time is _____

ATTORNEY

My attorney is _____

The location of his/her office is _____

The contact numbers are _____

My attorney's e-mail is _____

(4-B) COURT FEES AND RESTITUTION

I owe approximately $ _____.

I plan to pay the fee by (time frame) _____

These are the steps I need to do to pay my outstanding fee?

_____

_____

_____

_____

_____

These are the steps I need to do to prevent future fees?

_____

_____

_____

_____

_____

COURT FEES AND RESTITUTION

Current Balance: $ _____

$ _____	PAID ON _____	ENDING BALANCE	$ _____
$ _____	PAID ON _____	ENDING BALANCE	$ _____
$ _____	PAID ON _____	ENDING BALANCE	$ _____
$ _____	PAID ON _____	ENDING BALANCE	$ _____
$ _____	PAID ON _____	ENDING BALANCE	$ _____
$ _____	PAID ON _____	ENDING BALANCE	$ _____
$ _____	PAID ON _____	ENDING BALANCE	$ _____
$ _____	PAID ON _____	ENDING BALANCE	$ _____
$ _____	PAID ON _____	ENDING BALANCE	$ _____
$ _____	PAID ON _____	ENDING BALANCE	$ _____
$ _____	PAID ON _____	ENDING BALANCE	$ _____
$ _____	PAID ON _____	ENDING BALANCE	$ _____
$ _____	PAID ON _____	ENDING BALANCE	$ _____
$ _____	PAID ON _____	ENDING BALANCE	$ _____
$ _____	PAID ON _____	ENDING BALANCE	$ _____
$ _____	PAID ON _____	ENDING BALANCE	$ _____
$ _____	PAID ON _____	ENDING BALANCE	$ _____
$ _____	PAID ON _____	ENDING BALANCE	$ _____
$ _____	PAID ON _____	ENDING BALANCE	$ _____
$ _____	PAID ON _____	ENDING BALANCE	$ _____
$ _____	PAID ON _____	ENDING BALANCE	$ _____

(4-C) DRIVER'S LICENSE
DRIVING STATUS

What is the purpose of a driver's license?

_____

_____

_____

The nearest Secretary of State or Department of Motor Vehicle is located at

_____

_____

My current driver's status is… <u>active</u> <u>suspended</u>   <u>restricted</u>   <u>revoked</u>

If my response is anything other than **active**, I should complete the following…

What factors contributed to my driving privileges being suspended?

_____

_____

_____

These are the steps I need implement to re-establish my driving privileges?

_____

_____

_____

(4-D) UNPAID MOTOR VEHICLE TICKETS

(MOVING OR PARKED)

My outstanding balance is $ _____

My monthly payment is $ _____

What factors contributed to me acquiring motor vehicle tickets?

_____

_____

_____

_____

These are the steps I need to implement to pay my tickets.

_____

_____

_____

_____

These are the steps I need to implement to prevent future tickets.

_____

_____

_____

_____

UNPAID MOTOR VEHICLE FEES

Current Balance: $ _____

$ _____	PAID ON _____	ENDING BALANCE	$ _____
$ _____	PAID ON _____	ENDING BALANCE	$ _____
$ _____	PAID ON _____	ENDING BALANCE	$ _____
$ _____	PAID ON _____	ENDING BALANCE	$ _____
$ _____	PAID ON _____	ENDING BALANCE	$ _____
$ _____	PAID ON _____	ENDING BALANCE	$ _____
$ _____	PAID ON _____	ENDING BALANCE	$ _____
$ _____	PAID ON _____	ENDING BALANCE	$ _____
$ _____	PAID ON _____	ENDING BALANCE	$ _____
$ _____	PAID ON _____	ENDING BALANCE	$ _____
$ _____	PAID ON _____	ENDING BALANCE	$ _____
$ _____	PAID ON _____	ENDING BALANCE	$ _____
$ _____	PAID ON _____	ENDING BALANCE	$ _____
$ _____	PAID ON _____	ENDING BALANCE	$ _____
$ _____	PAID ON _____	ENDING BALANCE	$ _____
$ _____	PAID ON _____	ENDING BALANCE	$ _____
$ _____	PAID ON _____	ENDING BALANCE	$ _____
$ _____	PAID ON _____	ENDING BALANCE	$ _____
$ _____	PAID ON _____	ENDING BALANCE	$ _____
$ _____	PAID ON _____	ENDING BALANCE	$ _____
$ _____	PAID ON _____	ENDING BALANCE	$ _____

CONNECTING DOTS (4A-4D)

What does your picture look like in this area?

___

What did you learn about yourself?

What, if any, steps will you begin to implement to draw a different picture to improve this area of your life?

(4-E) OUTSTANDING INCOME TAXES

FEDERAL

My outstanding balance is $ _____

My monthly payment is $ _____

What factors contributed to me acquiring an outstanding balance in my income taxes?

_____

_____

_____

_____

These are the steps I need to implement to pay my taxes in full.

_____

_____

_____

_____

These are the steps I need to do to prevent owing taxes in the future.

_____

_____

_____

_____

FEDERAL INCOME TAXES

PAYMENT HISTORY

Current Balance: $ _____

$ _____	PAID ON _____	ENDING BALANCE	$ _____
$ _____	PAID ON _____	ENDING BALANCE	$ _____
$ _____	PAID ON _____	ENDING BALANCE	$ _____
$ _____	PAID ON _____	ENDING BALANCE	$ _____
$ _____	PAID ON _____	ENDING BALANCE	$ _____
$ _____	PAID ON _____	ENDING BALANCE	$ _____
$ _____	PAID ON _____	ENDING BALANCE	$ _____
$ _____	PAID ON _____	ENDING BALANCE	$ _____
$ _____	PAID ON _____	ENDING BALANCE	$ _____
$ _____	PAID ON _____	ENDING BALANCE	$ _____
$ _____	PAID ON _____	ENDING BALANCE	$ _____
$ _____	PAID ON _____	ENDING BALANCE	$ _____
$ _____	PAID ON _____	ENDING BALANCE	$ _____
$ _____	PAID ON _____	ENDING BALANCE	$ _____
$ _____	PAID ON _____	ENDING BALANCE	$ _____
$ _____	PAID ON _____	ENDING BALANCE	$ _____
$ _____	PAID ON _____	ENDING BALANCE	$ _____
$ _____	PAID ON _____	ENDING BALANCE	$ _____
$ _____	PAID ON _____	ENDING BALANCE	$ _____
$ _____	PAID ON _____	ENDING BALANCE	$ _____
$ _____	PAID ON _____	ENDING TAXES	$ _____

(4-E) OUTSTANDING INCOME TAXES

STATE

My outstanding balance is $ _____

My monthly payment is $ _____

What factors contributed to me acquiring an outstanding balance in my income taxes?

_____
_____
_____
_____

These are the steps I need to implement to pay my taxes in full.

_____
_____
_____
_____

These are the steps I need to implement to prevent owing taxes in the future.

_____
_____
_____
_____

STATE INCOME TAXES

PAYMENT HISTORY

Current Balance: $ _____

$ _____	PAID ON _____	ENDING BALANCE	$ _____
$ _____	PAID ON _____	ENDING BALANCE	$ _____
$ _____	PAID ON _____	ENDING BALANCE	$ _____
$ _____	PAID ON _____	ENDING BALANCE	$ _____
$ _____	PAID ON _____	ENDING BALANCE	$ _____
$ _____	PAID ON _____	ENDING BALANCE	$ _____
$ _____	PAID ON _____	ENDING BALANCE	$ _____
$ _____	PAID ON _____	ENDING BALANCE	$ _____
$ _____	PAID ON _____	ENDING BALANCE	$ _____
$ _____	PAID ON _____	ENDING BALANCE	$ _____
$ _____	PAID ON _____	ENDING BALANCE	$ _____
$ _____	PAID ON _____	ENDING BALANCE	$ _____
$ _____	PAID ON _____	ENDING BALANCE	$ _____
$ _____	PAID ON _____	ENDING BALANCE	$ _____
$ _____	PAID ON _____	ENDING BALANCE	$ _____
$ _____	PAID ON _____	ENDING BALANCE	$ _____
$ _____	PAID ON _____	ENDING BALANCE	$ _____
$ _____	PAID ON _____	ENDING BALANCE	$ _____
$ _____	PAID ON _____	ENDING BALANCE	$ _____
$ _____	PAID ON _____	ENDING BALANCE	$ _____
$ _____	PAID ON _____	ENDING BALANCE	$ _____

(4-E) OUTSTANDING INCOME TAXES

CITY

My outstanding balance is $ _____

My monthly payment is $ _____

What factors contributed to me acquiring an outstanding balance in my income taxes?

_____
_____
_____
_____

These are the steps I need to implement to pay my taxes in full.

_____
_____
_____
_____

These are the steps I need to implement to prevent owing taxes in the future.

_____
_____
_____
_____

CITY INCOME TAXES

PAYMENT HISTORY

Current Balance: $ _____

$ _____	PAID ON _____	ENDING BALANCE	$ _____
$ _____	PAID ON _____	ENDING BALANCE	$ _____
$ _____	PAID ON _____	ENDING BALANCE	$ _____
$ _____	PAID ON _____	ENDING BALANCE	$ _____
$ _____	PAID ON _____	ENDING BALANCE	$ _____
$ _____	PAID ON _____	ENDING BALANCE	$ _____
$ _____	PAID ON _____	ENDING BALANCE	$ _____
$ _____	PAID ON _____	ENDING BALANCE	$ _____
$ _____	PAID ON _____	ENDING BALANCE	$ _____
$ _____	PAID ON _____	ENDING BALANCE	$ _____
$ _____	PAID ON _____	ENDING BALANCE	$ _____
$ _____	PAID ON _____	ENDING BALANCE	$ _____
$ _____	PAID ON _____	ENDING BALANCE	$ _____
$ _____	PAID ON _____	ENDING BALANCE	$ _____
$ _____	PAID ON _____	ENDING BALANCE	$ _____
$ _____	PAID ON _____	ENDING BALANCE	$ _____
$ _____	PAID ON _____	ENDING BALANCE	$ _____
$ _____	PAID ON _____	ENDING BALANCE	$ _____
$ _____	PAID ON _____	ENDING BALANCE	$ _____
$ _____	PAID ON _____	ENDING BALANCE	$ _____

(4-F) PROPERTY TAXES

PRIMARY RESIDENCE

My outstanding balance is $ _____

My monthly payment is $ _____

What factors contributed to me acquiring an outstanding balance in my taxes?

_____

_____

_____

_____

These are the steps I need to implement to pay my taxes in full.

_____

_____

_____

_____

These are the steps I need to implement to prevent owing taxes in the future.

_____

_____

_____

_____

(4-F) PROPERTY TAXES

INVESTMENT PROPERTY

My outstanding balance is $ _____

My monthly payment is $ _____

What factors contributed to me acquiring an outstanding balance in my taxes?

_____
_____
_____
_____

These are the steps I need to implement to pay my taxes in full.

_____
_____
_____
_____

These are the steps I need to implement to prevent owing taxes in the future.

_____
_____
_____
_____

(4-G) OUTSTANDING CHILD SUPPORT

HOW MUCH DO I OWE MY CHILDREN?

MY CHILD SUPPORT STATUS IS …

    CURRENT   _____
    LATE   _____
    NEVER PAID   _____
    SUSPENDED   _____
    TERMINATED   _____

If my response is anything other than **current or terminated**, I should complete the following …

The nearest Friend of the Court is located at

_____

The contact number is _____

My outstanding balance is $ _____.

My monthly payment is $ _____.

I plan to re-establish my child support payments by (time frame)

_____

These are the steps I need to do to re-establish my child support payments.

_____

_____

_____

_____

CHILD SUPPORT

PAYMENT HISTORY

Current Balance: $ _____

$ _____	PAID ON _____	ENDING BALANCE	$ _____
$ _____	PAID ON _____	ENDING BALANCE	$ _____
$ _____	PAID ON _____	ENDING BALANCE	$ _____
$ _____	PAID ON _____	ENDING BALANCE	$ _____
$ _____	PAID ON _____	ENDING BALANCE	$ _____
$ _____	PAID ON _____	ENDING BALANCE	$ _____
$ _____	PAID ON _____	ENDING BALANCE	$ _____
$ _____	PAID ON _____	ENDING BALANCE	$ _____
$ _____	PAID ON _____	ENDING BALANCE	$ _____
$ _____	PAID ON _____	ENDING BALANCE	$ _____
$ _____	PAID ON _____	ENDING BALANCE	$ _____
$ _____	PAID ON _____	ENDING BALANCE	$ _____
$ _____	PAID ON _____	ENDING BALANCE	$ _____
$ _____	PAID ON _____	ENDING BALANCE	$ _____
$ _____	PAID ON _____	ENDING BALANCE	$ _____
$ _____	PAID ON _____	ENDING BALANCE	$ _____
$ _____	PAID ON _____	ENDING BALANCE	$ _____
$ _____	PAID ON _____	ENDING BALANCE	$ _____
$ _____	PAID ON _____	ENDING BALANCE	$ _____
$ _____	PAID ON _____	ENDING BALANCE	$ _____
$ _____	PAID ON _____	ENDING BALANCE	$ _____

(4-H) ALIMONY

HOW MUCH DO I OWE THE EX?

MY ALIMONY STATUS IS …

CURRENT   LATE   NEVER PAID   SUSPENDED   TERMINATED

If my response is anything other than **current or terminated**, I should complete the following…

The presiding judge over my divorce is named …

_____

My divorce attorney is named _____

The location of his/her office is _____

The contact number is _____

The e-mail address is _____

My outstanding balance is $ _____.

My monthly payment is $ _____.

I plan to re-establish my alimony payments by (time frame)

_____

The steps I need to do to re-establish my alimony payments.

_____

_____

_____

24 – MONTH ALIMONY

PAYMENT HISTORY

Current Balance: $ _____

$ _____	PAID ON _____	ENDING BALANCE	$ _____
$ _____	PAID ON _____	ENDING BALANCE	$ _____
$ _____	PAID ON _____	ENDING BALANCE	$ _____
$ _____	PAID ON _____	ENDING BALANCE	$ _____
$ _____	PAID ON _____	ENDING BALANCE	$ _____
$ _____	PAID ON _____	ENDING BALANCE	$ _____
$ _____	PAID ON _____	ENDING BALANCE	$ _____
$ _____	PAID ON _____	ENDING BALANCE	$ _____
$ _____	PAID ON _____	ENDING BALANCE	$ _____
$ _____	PAID ON _____	ENDING BALANCE	$ _____
$ _____	PAID ON _____	ENDING BALANCE	$ _____
$ _____	PAID ON _____	ENDING BALANCE	$ _____
$ _____	PAID ON _____	ENDING BALANCE	$ _____
$ _____	PAID ON _____	ENDING BALANCE	$ _____
$ _____	PAID ON _____	ENDING BALANCE	$ _____
$ _____	PAID ON _____	ENDING BALANCE	$ _____
$ _____	PAID ON _____	ENDING BALANCE	$ _____
$ _____	PAID ON _____	ENDING BALANCE	$ _____
$ _____	PAID ON _____	ENDING BALANCE	$ _____
$ _____	PAID ON _____	ENDING BALANCE	$ _____
$ _____	PAID ON _____	ENDING BALANCE	$ _____
$ _____	PAID ON _____	ENDING BALANCE	$ _____
$ _____	PAID ON _____	ENDING BALANCE	$ _____
$ _____	PAID ON _____	ENDING BALANCE	$ _____

(4-I) HUMAN SERVICES

My social worker is _____

The name of the agency is _____

The location is _____

The contact number is _____

My social worker's e-mail is _____

My report date and time is _____

My case manager is _____

The name of the agency is _____

The location is _____

The contact number is _____

My case manager's e-mail is _____

My report date and time is _____

My foster care worker is _____

The name of the agency is _____

The location is _____

The contact number is _____

My foster care's e-mail is _____

My report date and time is _____

CONNECTING DOTS (4E-I)

What does your picture look like in this area?

_____
_____
_____
_____
_____
_____
_____
_____
_____

What did you learn about yourself?

_____
_____
_____
_____
_____
_____
_____
_____
_____
_____

What, if any, steps will you begin to implement to draw a different picture to improve this area of your life?

DOT #5

MEDICAL

WHAT IS MY BODY REALLY SAYING?

DOT #5-A   DIFFERENT LEVELS OF CARE

DOT #5-B   MY PHYSICAL HEALTH COVERAGE

DOT #5-C   TRACKING MY SURGERIES

DOT #5-D   TRACKING MY OFFICE VISITS

DOT #5-E   TRACKING MY MEDICATIONS

DOT #5-F   TRACKING MY DAILY DOSAGES

DOT #5-G   MY DENTAL COVERAGE

DOT #5-H   TRACKING MY DENTAL VISITS

DIFFERENT LEVELS OF CARE

What is "Outpatient Services"?

_____
_____
_____
_____

What is "Urgent Care Services"?

_____
_____
_____
_____

What is "Emergency Services"?

_____
_____
_____
_____

What is "Hospitalization Services"?

_____
_____
_____
_____

What is the purpose/function of Health Insurance?

What is the purpose/function of Medicare?

What is the purpose/function of Medicaid?

MY PHYSICAL HEALTH COVERAGE

My health insurance is _____

My contract number is _____

My coverage includes _____

My co-pay for office visits is $_____ per visit.

My co-pay for prescription drugs is $_____.

My primary care physician is _____

The location is _____

Contact number is _____

My health concerns are …

_____

_____

_____

_____

My physical exercise/regiment consists of …

_____

_____

_____

_____

_____

TRACKING MY SURGERIES

<u>DATE</u>

_____ REASON: _____

_____ REASON: _____

_____ REASON: _____

_____ REASON: _____

_____ REASON: _____

_____ REASON: _____

_____ REASON: _____

_____ REASON: _____

_____ REASON: _____

_____ REASON: _____

_____ REASON: _____

_____ REASON: _____

_____ REASON: _____

_____ REASON: _____

_____ REASON: _____

_____ REASON: _____

_____ REASON: _____

_____ REASON: _____

_____ REASON: _____

_____ REASON: _____

_____ REASON: _____

_____ REASON: _____

TRACKING MY OFFICE VISITS

<u>DATE</u>

_____	REASON: _____	CO-PAY $ _____
_____	REASON: _____	CO-PAY $ _____
_____	REASON: _____	CO-PAY $ _____
_____	REASON: _____	CO-PAY $ _____
_____	REASON: _____	CO-PAY $ _____
_____	REASON: _____	CO-PAY $ _____
_____	REASON: _____	CO-PAY $ _____
_____	REASON: _____	CO-PAY $ _____
_____	REASON: _____	CO-PAY $ _____
_____	REASON: _____	CO-PAY $ _____
_____	REASON: _____	CO-PAY $ _____
_____	REASON: _____	CO-PAY $ _____
_____	REASON: _____	CO-PAY $ _____
_____	REASON: _____	CO-PAY $ _____
_____	REASON: _____	CO-PAY $ _____
_____	REASON: _____	CO-PAY $ _____
_____	REASON: _____	CO-PAY $ _____
_____	REASON: _____	CO-PAY $ _____
_____	REASON: _____	CO-PAY $ _____
_____	REASON: _____	CO-PAY $ _____
_____	REASON: _____	CO-PAY $ _____

TRACKING MY MEDICATIONS

DATE PRESCRIBED	NAME	REASON

TRACKING MY DAILY DOSAGES

TIME　　　　　　　　NAMES OF MEDICATION　　　　　　　　DOSAGE/FREQUENCY

MY DENTAL COVERAGE

My dental health insurance is _____

My contract number is _____

My coverage includes _____

My co-pay for dental visits are $_____ per visit.

My dentist is _____

The location is _____

Contact number is _____

My dental concerns are …

_____

_____

_____

_____

_____

My dental regiment consists of …

_____

_____

_____

_____

_____

TRACKING MY DENTAL VISITS

DATE

DATE		
_____	REASON: _____	CO-PAY $ _____
_____	REASON: _____	CO-PAY $ _____
_____	REASON: _____	CO-PAY $ _____
_____	REASON: _____	CO-PAY $ _____
_____	REASON: _____	CO-PAY $ _____
_____	REASON: _____	CO-PAY $ _____
_____	REASON: _____	CO-PAY $ _____
_____	REASON: _____	CO-PAY $ _____
_____	REASON: _____	CO-PAY $ _____
_____	REASON: _____	CO-PAY $ _____
_____	REASON: _____	CO-PAY $ _____
_____	REASON: _____	CO-PAY $ _____
_____	REASON: _____	CO-PAY $ _____
_____	REASON: _____	CO-PAY $ _____
_____	REASON: _____	CO-PAY $ _____
_____	REASON: _____	CO-PAY $ _____
_____	REASON: _____	CO-PAY $ _____
_____	REASON: _____	CO-PAY $ _____
_____	REASON: _____	CO-PAY $ _____
_____	REASON: _____	CO-PAY $ _____
_____	REASON: _____	CO-PAY $ _____
_____	REASON: _____	CO-PAY $ _____

CONNECTING DOTS (5A- 5H)

What does your picture look like in this area?

What did you learn about yourself?

What, if any, steps will you begin to implement to draw a different picture to improve this area of your life?

ABOUT THE AUTHOR

Eric is a native of Detroit, Michigan and matriculated through the Detroit Public School System. Eric attended Murray-Wright Senior High School and was a cadet in the Naval Junior Reserve Officers Training Corp; more commonly known as N.J.R.O.T.C. At the end of his Junior Year, Eric was promoted to Executive Officer, the second highest student in command of the entire battalion. However, his highest achievement in high school occurred when his senior class had elected him to become their Senior Class President in 1990.

Eric graduated from high school and continued to pursue higher education at Wilberforce University located in Wilberforce, Ohio. Wilberforce University is the oldest, private historical black college in the United States and founded in 1856 by the A.M.E. church. Wilberforce University was named for the famous abolitionist William Wilberforce. In addition, Wilberforce University was a vital part of the Underground Railroad and it is in close proximity to the historical Payne Theological Seminary in which many clergy men received their degrees and ultimately participated in the Civil Rights Movement.

Eric participated in numerous student organizations during his matriculation at Wilberforce University. However, one of his highest achievements occurred when he was selected to become a member of Omega Psi Phi Fraternity, Upsilon Chapter founded by the Honorable Colonel Charles H. Young, the third African-American officer who attended West Point Military Academy. Eric earned his Bachelor of Arts Degree in Political Science in 1994.

Eric further pursued higher education by attending Wayne State University Graduate School located in Detroit, Michigan. Eric was accepted to the Counseling Education Program in 1995 and earned his Master of Arts Degree in Counseling Education specializing in mental health and community counseling in 1998. Eric is a highly skilled mental health practitioner and clinical psychotherapist. In addition, Eric is the co-founder of Eason Counseling and Consulting, an agency that provides counseling and consulting services to various businesses and non profit organizations. Eric has counseled thousands of people on various issues throughout the years, hence the origin of Connecting-The-Dots.

Finally, Eric is a licensed minister of the Gospel of Jesus Christ and believes in the power of the Holy Spirit. Eric's personal motto is "It is not where you start, but where you finish!"

www.ingramcontent.com/pod-product-compliance
Lightning Source LLC
Chambersburg PA
CBHW080734230426
43665CB00020B/2731